SO-AAB-378

PROS AND CONS

# THE DEBATE ABOUT LEGALIZING
# MARIJUANA

by Marne Ventura

FOCUS
READERS

# FOCUS READERS

## www.focusreaders.com

Focus Readers is distributed by North Star Editions:
sales@northstareditions.com | 888-417-0195

Produced for Focus Readers by Red Line Editorial.

Photographs ©: OpenRangeStock/iStockphoto, cover, 1; Canna Obscura/Shutterstock Images, 4–5; Red Line Editorial, 7, 25; Alexander Mazurkevich/Shutterstock Images, 8–9; Roxana Gonzalez/Shutterstock Images, 11; Steve Heap/Shutterstock Images, 13; AlenaPaulus/iStockphoto, 14–15; Humpback_Whale/Shutterstock Images, 17; David Maska/Shutterstock Images, 19; wellphoto/Shutterstock Images, 20–21; Joshua Rainey Photography/Shutterstock Images, 23, 44; KatarzynaBialasiewicz/iStockphoto, 26–27; aastock/Shutterstock Images, 28; Dan Holm/Shutterstock Images, 31; RichLegg/iStockphoto, 32–33, 45; David Zalubowski/AP Images, 35; KellyNelson/Shutterstock Images, 37; Lester Balajadia/Shutterstock Images, 38–39; Kaesler Media/Shutterstock Images, 40; Lillydawg/Shutterstock Images, 43

### ISBN
978-1-63517-522-6 (hardcover)
978-1-63517-594-3 (paperback)
978-1-63517-738-1 (ebook pdf)
978-1-63517-666-7 (hosted ebook)

### Library of Congress Control Number: 2017948095

Printed in the United States of America
Mankato, MN
November, 2017

## ABOUT THE AUTHOR

Marne Ventura is the author of more than 50 books for kids, both nonfiction and fiction. A former elementary school teacher, Marne holds a master's degree in education from the University of California. She and her husband live on the central coast of California.

# TABLE OF CONTENTS

# CHAPTER 1

# THE BASICS OF MARIJUANA

Humans have used marijuana since ancient times. Farmers in Central Asia and India grew marijuana thousands of years ago. Today, marijuana is grown all over the world.

Marijuana is the name for the dried leaves and flowers of the cannabis plant. Cannabis plants contain more than 400 chemicals. These chemicals have many uses. For example, doctors **prescribe** medical marijuana to treat pain.

**Growers dry marijuana plants by hanging them upside down.**

Some people use marijuana for **recreational** purposes. They might smoke a marijuana cigarette or eat foods containing marijuana. Chemicals in marijuana can make users feel happy and relaxed. This feeling is called a high.

Laws on marijuana vary around the world. Uruguay legalized marijuana use in 2013. In Japan, the punishment for using marijuana is up to five years in prison. According to US federal law, use or possession of marijuana is illegal. Still, many US states have legalized some forms of the drug. Technically, state laws cannot go against federal laws. But as of 2017, federal officials have not stopped states from legalizing marijuana.

Peoples' opinions about marijuana differ greatly. Some people believe all marijuana use is dangerous. They think the drug should be illegal. Others believe marijuana should be legal for medical use only. Some people want to legalize both medical and recreational marijuana.

Americans who use marijuana in states where it is legal are still breaking the federal law. For this reason, supporters of marijuana want to legalize it at both the federal and state levels.

## US MARIJUANA LAWS BY STATE (2017) ◄

CANADA

PACIFIC OCEAN

ATLANTIC OCEAN

MEXICO

**Marijuana Legalization Status**

◼ Medical marijuana broadly legalized
◼ Marijuana legalized for recreational use
◼ No broad laws legalizing marijuana

# CHAPTER 2

# PRO
# MARIJUANA HAS
# MEDICAL VALUE

Medical marijuana can take several forms. Some examples are cigarettes, sprays, oils, and lotions. THC and CBD are chemicals in marijuana. THC changes how the brain works, causing the user to feel high. In contrast, CBD does not cause a high.

In many cases, the chemicals in marijuana can help patients feel better. For instance, cancer patients often deal with nausea and tiredness.

**Bhang milk is an Indian drink made with marijuana. It is often used for healing purposes.**

These symptoms are caused by **chemotherapy.**
Some patients don't feel like eating. Doctors
may prescribe marijuana in these cases. THC can
stop nausea and increase patients' appetites.
According to animal studies, THC and CBD can
slow down and kill certain cancer cells. However,
scientists have not done enough human studies to
know marijuana's true effects against cancer.

## ➤ FDA APPROVAL

The US Food and Drug Administration (FDA) must
approve all drugs in the United States. Researchers test
drugs on hundreds of people before they are approved.
These tests show whether a drug is helpful, harmful, or
both. In 1972, the US government identified marijuana
as a dangerous drug. This ruling made it difficult for
researchers to fund studies on marijuana. The ruling
also made it hard to obtain marijuana for research.

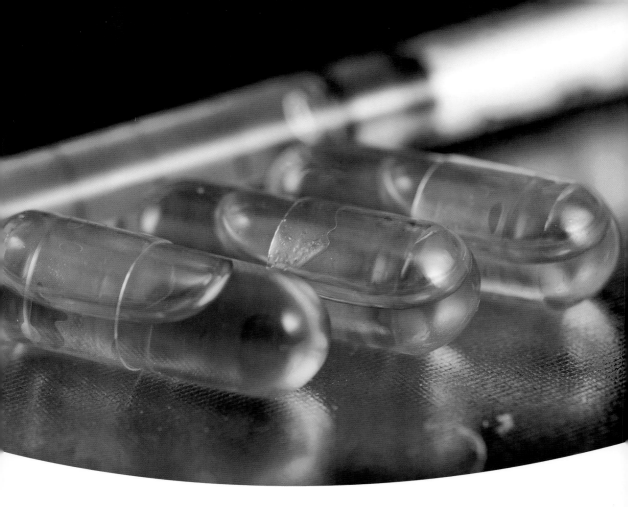

⬆ CBD oil often comes in the form of capsules.

Doctors also use medical marijuana to treat epilepsy. Epilepsy is a disorder that causes seizures. When people have seizures, they lose control of their muscles. This can cause patients to fall and hurt themselves.

Frequent seizures can make it hard to live a normal life. Many drugs are intended to stop seizures, but they don't always work. Some patients have turned to marijuana for treatment. To treat epilepsy, scientists make CBD oil from marijuana plants. Studies show that a drug made from CBD oil can reduce seizures.

For pain relief, marijuana may be a safer alternative to **opiates**. Doctors often prescribe opiates to treat pain. However, opiates can have dangerous side effects. They can cause liver damage, brain damage, and stomach problems. In time, patients need stronger doses of opiates to relieve their pain. This can cause users to become **addicted**. They can even die from taking too large a dose. More than 33,000 people died from opioid overdose in 2015. Nearly half of these deaths were from prescription drugs.

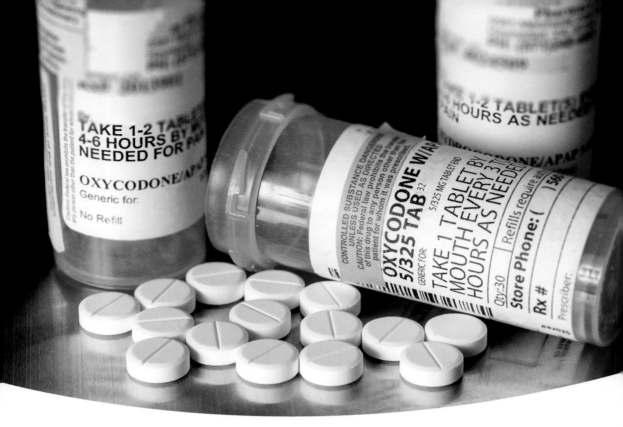

Some opiates, such as oxycodone (above), are legal in the United States. Others, such as heroin, are illegal.

Studies on THC show that marijuana eases many types of pain. In 2016, doctors prescribed 1,800 fewer painkillers in states where medical marijuana was legal. And a 2014 study found that opiate overdose deaths fell by 25 percent in states with legal medical marijuana. Medical marijuana does not carry the risk of death by overdose.

# CHAPTER 3

# PRO
# LEGAL MARIJUANA CAN GENERATE GOVERNMENT INCOME

Governments use tax money to pay for public services. These services include police officers, judges, and prison workers. Arrests related to marijuana increase the need for such services. In the United States, for example, nearly half of all drug charges are related to marijuana. And each year, more than 800,000 Americans are arrested for using or possessing marijuana.

Morocco, Afghanistan, and Mexico are some of the world's top marijuana producers.

Legalizing marijuana could save US taxpayers nearly $8 billion per year.

Governments spend a lot of money fighting marijuana. By legalizing the drug, governments could create extra income instead. Experts estimate that the marijuana industry generates up to $40 billion per year in the United States. But much of this money goes to illegal drug dealers. Supporters of legalization argue that money from marijuana sales should go to legal farmers and sellers. It could also go to the government.

Normally, business owners pay taxes to the government. These funds help cover workers' retirement and health care plans. But when people buy and sell marijuana illegally, none of that money is taxed. Experts estimate that state taxes from legal marijuana could generate between $5 and $18 billion per year.

▲ Legal marijuana sales would cut into the profit of illegal dealers.

Taxes from marijuana sales would allow governments to increase their spending. The US state of Colorado is one example. In 2012, Colorado legalized recreational marijuana. In 2016, the state earned nearly $200 million from taxes on the drug.

State officials in Colorado used the extra money to benefit citizens. They repaired old schools and built new ones. They also created educational programs to stop bullying. Other programs educated young people on the dangers of drug use. The state also provided money to the Colorado Department of Agriculture (CDA). The CDA used the funds to increase safety on marijuana farms.

In 2001 and 2003, 38 percent of surveyed adults said they tried marijuana. In a 2013 survey, that number rose to 48 percent. Supporters of legalization point out that marijuana use is on the

> ## ➤ DID YOU KNOW?

In 2012, Colorado and Washington became the first US states to legalize recreational marijuana. Alaska, Oregon, and Washington, DC, followed in 2014.

▲ The CDA prevents marijuana growers from spraying plants with certain dangerous chemicals.

rise. This shows that laws against marijuana do not prevent marijuana use. Legalizing marijuana would save taxpayer money. It could also create more funds for drug safety programs.

# CHAPTER 4

# PRO
# LAW ENFORCEMENT COULD FOCUS ON VIOLENT CRIMES

Police officers serve an important role in the community. Their job is to protect citizens and enforce laws. Some people argue that officers spend too much time enforcing laws against marijuana. These critics want police to spend more time protecting citizens against violent crimes. If marijuana were legal, growers, sellers, and users would not be breaking the law. Officers could spend less time enforcing marijuana laws.

**Illegal dealers must secretly transport marijuana to avoid being caught.**

This would give them more time to protect people from violence.

Violent crime causes physical harm to another person. Examples include murder, armed robbery, and assault. In contrast, responsible use of marijuana does not harm others. Many people consider marijuana use a victimless crime. These individuals want the police to focus on crimes that have victims.

## ➤ MARIJUANA ARRESTS IN THE UNITED STATES

Between 2001 and 2010, US police arrested more than 8.2 million people for marijuana-related crimes. Of these arrests, approximately 90 percent were for possession of the drug. In 2011, more arrests occurred for marijuana possession in the United States than for all violent crimes combined.

In states where marijuana is legal, marijuana dispensaries provide medical marijuana to the public.

Legalizing marijuana would also allow the government to **regulate** the marijuana industry. In states where it is legal, marijuana is sold in state-regulated shops. This means the state can control its growth, sales, and use. In Colorado, users must show identification to buy marijuana. Legal cannabis is grown on state-approved farms.

This allows the government to oversee the quality of the drug. It also reduces crime connected to the illegal drug trade.

In contrast, laws against marijuana can result in dangerous industry practices. In addition, illegal transportation of the drug across the Mexican–US border causes other crimes. Violence can occur among marijuana sellers. Users may steal money so they can buy the drug. A 2017 study found that legalizing marijuana reduces such crime. US medical marijuana laws have led to less violence in states that border Mexico.

According to US federal law, the penalty for marijuana possession is one year in jail. Penalties for selling and growing marijuana are at least five years in jail. First-time marijuana users are put into jail with other criminals. This experience can negatively affect them. Their peers may influence them to commit more crimes in the future. After **inmates** are released, it is difficult to return to normal life. Nearly half of all inmates return to prison after being released. People with criminal records also have trouble finding jobs. Supporters of legalizing marijuana argue that there are ways other than jail to help people with drug problems.

## US FEDERAL PENALTIES FOR MARIJUANA-RELATED CRIMES ◄

| | Maximum prison sentence | Maximum fine |
|---|---|---|
| **Possession** | | |
| Any amount (first offense) | 1 year | $1,000 |
| Any amount (second offense) | 2 years | $2,500 |
| Any amount (third offense) | 3 years | $5,000 |
| **Sale* or Cultivation** | | |
| Less than 50 kg | 5 years | $250,000 |
| 50–99 kg | 20 years | $1,000,000 |
| 100–999 kg | 40 years | $2,000,000 |
| 1000+ kg | life | $4,000,000 |

* Sales to a minor or within 1,000 feet (305 m) of a school carry a double penalty.

# CHAPTER 5

# CON MARIJUANA IS HARMFUL TO MINORS

In states where recreational marijuana is legal, users must be at least 21 years old. Adults in these states make their own decisions about using the drug. Critics of legalization argue that this sends the wrong message to **minors**. They fear that young people will be influenced by adults' marijuana use. Minors might think it is okay for them to use the drug, too.

**Marijuana is one of the most common drugs used by teenagers.**

FOR MEDICAL USE ONLY

NOT FOR CONSUMPTION
OF MINORS

SKUNK HAZE Cannbis Sativa Hybrid
Skunk No. 1 x Original Haze
THC: 22.7399%   CBD: 0.1418%

Any person who takes possesion or otherwise damages the materials
on these premises will be subject to felony.

Many marijuana sellers use warning labels to prevent use by minors.

Recreational marijuana poses many threats to minors. In the short term, THC impairs users' attention and memory. These effects can be dangerous. For instance, driving or biking while high can lead to accidents. THC also impairs users' decision-making abilities. Young people who are high might be more easily influenced by their peers. They might drink alcohol or use tobacco in response to peer pressure. Students who use marijuana might have trouble studying as well. This can affect their performance in school.

Young adults who use marijuana also risk long-term brain damage. Researchers in New Zealand tracked 1,000 people for 20 years. The participants reported their marijuana use at ages 18, 21, 26, 32, and 38. The people who used marijuana during three or more of the periods lost an average of six points on an **IQ test**.

## DID YOU KNOW? ◁

By age five or six, 95 percent of a child's brain is fully developed. The area that controls memory and mood continues to grow during a person's teenage years.

Researchers have linked teen marijuana use to other problems. For instance, many users have low grades in school. As a result, some users do not finish high school or go to college. Others have trouble finding a job. Opponents of legalization argue that marijuana use negatively affects these teens' futures.

Not all teenagers are aware of the effects of marijuana. When marijuana is legal, minors are less likely to think it is harmful. In Washington, researchers tracked teenagers' views on marijuana before and after legalization. Tenth graders' perception of the drug's harm fell by 16 percent. Parents worry that widespread legalization would have a similar effect.

Parents also worry about young children's access to marijuana. In places where marijuana is legal, the drug may be easier for minors to

Some people eat foods containing marijuana for medical purposes.

obtain. Recreational marijuana comes in many forms. Cookies, brownies, candies, and drinks can all be made with THC. These forms of marijuana are called **edibles**. Young children may mistake marijuana edibles for regular treats. If they accidentally eat them, children could become sick.

# CHAPTER 6

# CON
# DRIVING UNDER THE INFLUENCE
# OF MARIJUANA IS DANGEROUS

**M**ore than 37,000 US citizens die in auto accidents each year. And nearly 2.4 million people are injured in crashes. Driving under the influence of any drug is illegal. Many people argue that legalizing marijuana would lead to more accidents.

THC harms users' judgment, coordination, and reaction times. These effects make driving unsafe.

Driving under the influence of alcohol or drugs puts others' lives in danger.

THC is the second-most-common drug found in blood tests of crashed drivers. A driver under the influence of THC is approximately twice as likely as a sober driver to cause a deadly accident. Scientists say the exact role of marijuana in auto accidents is unclear. But critics of legalization believe enough evidence connects marijuana use with car accidents.

In 2015, drunk drivers caused approximately one-third of car accident deaths in the United States. These statistics show that drunk driving is very dangerous. Driving under the influence of both alcohol and THC is even more dangerous. When people use marijuana and drink alcohol at the same time, more THC enters the blood. Legalizing marijuana would make it easier for drivers to combine the two drugs. Some people fear this would lead to more accidents.

▲ Colorado's "Drive High, Get a DUI" campaign warns drivers of drugged driving.

In places where marijuana is illegal, people typically use marijuana in secret. They tend to stay home to avoid the police. Using marijuana at home helps keep the public safe. Some worry that this would change with legalization. People might be more likely to use marijuana outside of their homes. This would increase their likelihood of driving under the influence.

Legalizing marijuana would also make it harder to enforce safe driving. Identifying drivers who are under the influence of THC can be difficult. Sometimes, police officers smell or see marijuana in the car. But other times, signs of marijuana are not obvious. The driver might have smoked the marijuana in a different location. Or he or she might have eaten an edible form of the drug.

## ➤ CONFLICTING REPORTS

The US state of Washington legalized recreational marijuana in 2012. One study showed that deaths from marijuana-related crashes rose by nearly 50 percent between 2013 and 2014. However, another study found that deaths from marijuana-related crashes in Colorado and Washington did not increase. People on both sides of the argument agree that more research is needed.

⚐ Officers may use trained police dogs to detect marijuana in vehicles.

Officers must bring drivers to the police station to test for THC. However, the results of these tests are not always helpful. The drivers' THC levels can drop by the time they take the test. Police departments are searching for better ways to identify drivers under the influence of THC. Critics of legalization consider this a reason to keep marijuana illegal.

NO
SMOKING

# CHAPTER 7

# CON
# MARIJUANA USE LEADS TO MORE HARMFUL DRUG ABUSE

Some experts believe marijuana is a gateway drug. Gateway drugs lead users to use more dangerous drugs. Examples of gateway drugs include alcohol and **nicotine**. Most people don't start off using heroin or cocaine. These are extremely dangerous substances. More often, drug users begin with a beer or cigarette. After that, they might try some form of marijuana.

Gateway drugs, such as cigarettes, may seem harmless to users at first.

▲ Crystal meth is one of the most dangerous drugs.

In time, users become used to feeling high. Then they may turn to stronger drugs.

Research shows that most high school students who use illegal drugs tried marijuana first. The effects of THC may make other drugs more attractive to teens. But studies also show that many teens who try marijuana don't try other drugs. Therefore, marijuana does not always act as a gateway drug. Still, opponents of legalization think the risk is too high. They want to prevent teens from trying more harmful drugs.

Marijuana has different effects on different people. Smoking marijuana makes some people feel good. Others don't like the way it makes them feel. Studies show that people who regularly use marijuana often feel sad or worried. These individuals lose their desire for work and play.

## DID YOU KNOW? ◁

Most US teenagers do not try marijuana. However, one in six people who start using as teens becomes addicted, according to the National Institute on Drug Abuse.

They may feel bad about themselves. To feel better, they might try stronger drugs. Critics of legalization want to prevent this from happening.

Social factors also cause marijuana to act as a gateway drug. People who try marijuana may have friends who use other drugs. These friends might encourage marijuana users to try more dangerous substances. This could lead them to form unhealthy addictions.

Some studies of gateway drugs look at cigarettes, alcohol, and marijuana at the same time. This makes it hard to know the effects of marijuana alone. Therefore, researchers are not positive that marijuana is a gateway drug. Other factors could be involved. Still, there is a **correlation** between marijuana use and more harmful drug abuse. Research shows that young people who use cocaine and heroin usually use

▲ Peer pressure can lead teens to try drugs they wouldn't otherwise try.

marijuana as well. Because of this pattern, many people argue that marijuana is bad for public health.

# PROS

- Medical marijuana can ease side effects of chemotherapy and symptoms of epilepsy.
- Marijuana is a safe alternative to more dangerous painkillers.
- Legalizing marijuana would help governments cut spending on law enforcement.
- The government could use taxes from legal marijuana sales to benefit the public.
- Legalizing marijuana would allow police officers to focus on violent crimes.
- Legalizing marijuana would protect users from the negative effects of prison.

# CONS

- Recreational marijuana negatively affects physical and mental development.
- If marijuana were legal, more children might accidentally eat marijuana edibles.
- THC impairs users' ability to drive, causing more car crashes.
- Drinking alcohol while using marijuana causes more THC to enter the blood.
- Most teenagers who use illegal drugs used marijuana first.
- Marijuana users may turn to stronger drugs for increased effects.

# LEGALIZING MARIJUANA

*Write your answers on a separate piece of paper.*

1. Write a summary of the effects of recreational marijuana on young adults.

2. Are you for or against legalizing recreational marijuana? Why?

3. Which chemical from a cannabis plant makes users feel high?

    **A.** CBD
    **B.** opiates
    **C.** THC

4. What would be most likely to happen if marijuana were used for pain relief instead of opiates?

    **A.** Patients would become heavily addicted to marijuana.
    **B.** Patients would be less likely to die of overdose.
    **C.** Patients would experience no pain relief.

*Answer key on page 48.*

# GLOSSARY

**addicted**
Having a physical need to use a drug regularly.

**chemotherapy**
The use of chemical substances to kill cancer cells.

**correlation**
A relationship between one thing and another.

**edibles**
Things that can be eaten.

**inmates**
People who are confined to a prison.

**IQ test**
A test that measures a person's level of intelligence.

**minors**
People under the age of official adulthood and legal responsibility.

**nicotine**
A toxic and addictive drug that is found in tobacco.

**opiates**
Drugs made from an opium poppy plant.

**prescribe**
To recommend a treatment or medication to someone who is sick.

**recreational**
Done for fun and enjoyment.

**regulate**
To control or maintain.

# TO LEARN MORE

## BOOKS

Collins, Anna. *Marijuana: Abuse and Legalization*. Detroit: Lucent Press, 2017.

Goldstein, Margaret J. *Legalizing Marijuana: Promises and Pitfalls*. Minneapolis: Twenty-First Century Books, 2016.

Waters, Rosa. *Marijuana: Legal & Developmental Consequences*. Broomall, PA: Mason Crest, 2014.

## NOTE TO EDUCATORS

Visit **www.focusreaders.com** to find lesson plans, activities, links, and other resources related to this title.

# INDEX

**Answer Key: 1.** Answers will vary; **2.** Answers will vary; **3.** C; **4.** B